To Bill & Holly!

Hope you enjoy.

All the very best,

All Bowed Up!

MECHE'S MUSINGS

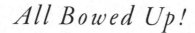

SHANE MECHE

DEDICATION

This book is dedicated to my beautiful children, Marina, Olivia, and Augustus. It is my sincere hope that you may one day find value in the words that I have written and share it with others in your life.

May you find in it my humor, guidance, passion, and other tidbits that cause you to pause for thought as well as inspire you to share your own insights with future generations.

CONTENTS

INTRODUCTION

"In this book you will find snippets of wisdom and foolishness; some contrived under Bourbon, some from a great cigar, but certainly a few with both!"

As a younger man, I always fancied the thought of writing a book of my own and have it published. Ideas, story lines, and grand tales were imagined that could be crafted into a work of fiction.

Alas, none of them really struck that cord of intense passion required to dedicate the time and energy needed to produce such a work. While those countless thoughts never flowed from ideas to paper, my notion of life's lessons, worldly advice, and odd bits of humor were however jotted down.

When I wrote "Labor of Love" it became the signature used on all email correspondence. Surprisingly, this struck a quite cord by many who were compelled to write and let me know not only did they love it, but what it meant to them personally. This, of course, inspired a continued effort of putting more thoughts into words.

It dawned on me one day that all of those bits written over the years had become quite the collection. Unknowingly, that dream of my own book had materialized in an unwitting manner. No longer should those words be kept to myself, but organized into a work that could perhaps benefit others.

POETRY

A NEW DAY

The sun has not yet risen
though the air is full of promise for a new day.

Yesterday is only a memory now,
back in my mind far, far away!

I look not yet for tomorrow,
though I know it will come.

It is the gift of today that I anticipate;
a new harvest of memories
soon to be yesterday.

With yesterday in the past,
and tomorrow in the future,
the only sure thing is the time of now!

Now I see the sun rising!

Yet another beautiful day!

❧

MI LUNA

"In the hustle and bustle
of souls abound,
slowly she rises thru the night
shining her ominous beauty,

yet few will notice
the obvious brilliance above
impacting their every move."

❦

AN ODE TO DR. SEUSS

Monday - Work Day!

Tuesday - Good Day!

Wednesday - Hump Day!

Thursday - Happy Day!

Friday - *Last Day!*

Saturday - pLaY DaY!

Sunday - GOD'S Day!

ADVICE

ADVICE

❧

BE YOURSELF

"The message to my children is to
live and love with no regrets.

Let not the **judgment** of others define
the person who you will **become,**
instead live a **life** of one that
inspires others to
be more like
yourself."

BE LEADERS

"Be leaders

in everything you do,

though never forget to

learn lessons from those

who have preceded you. "

❧

CONSEQUENCE

"Choosing to do the right thing is easy.
The consequences however can be challenging."

A BETTER MAN

"No man has ever grown to become a better person
by surrounding himself only
with like-minded
people."

BE DIFFERENT

"Dare to be different,

but remember to respect others

when doing so."

❦

COMPLIMENT

"The graceful acceptance of a
compliment is much more genuine

than any acknowledgement
from one expecting praise."

LESSER OF EVILS

"Never choose between the

lesser of two evils,

instead select the one where you can leave

a positive impact."

PEOPLE IN YOUR LIFE

"Friends are made, family inherited.

Only you can choose the importance

each plays in your life."

❧

TRUE FRIEND

"To befriend another without

expectation or need of reciprocation

spares one of ever being

disappointed with the outcome."

CROWD

"In times of panic or peril,

never follow the crowd

as they are almost always wrong."

DEBT

"Debt is life's
double edge sword.

Learn to use it wisely
lest it's cuts will bleed you!"

LOVE

❧

IMPERFECT MAN

"I am an imperfect man, and try as I may, I don't seem to have the capacity to love completely and unconditionally as only a woman can."

❧

PERFECT MOMENTS

"You are many perfect moments

in time on my

journey in life!"

CHOOSING LOVE

"Of course I would, but love is a strange thing,
we don't get to choose it.

It just happens, and rarely with who
we think it should be with.

The heart has no eyes or purse,
it loves unconditionally."

RELATIONSHIP

"The very best of a man shows as a
reflection of the woman he is with.

When each look in the mirror and see the other,
that's what makes things work!"

❧

UNCONDITIONAL

"**I**f you give your heart unconditionally,
then you are never disappointed!"

❧

SUPERPOWER

"Every person has two superpowers:
love and forgiveness,

both of which can be given
freely and neither denied."

❦

OF TRUST

"The presence of a strong man in the life of an independent woman in love allows the ease of her defenses to the lady she was meant to be."

HUMOR

HUMOR

⚜

ACHIEVING CLARITY

"If you are having trouble

expressing yourself,

clarity can be achieved with

a bit of Bourbon!"

CIGAR DAYS

"For some men cigars are

for a good day,

or bad day,

a great day,

or sad day."

"I prefer my cigars

every day!"

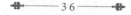

FRANKINCHURN

DEFINITION:
fran·kin·churn
/ˈfraŋ-kin-chərn/
verb

    1. "the act of speaking one's mind causing loss of friend-ship while simultaneously gaining others."

❧

INSPIRATION

*"In this book you will find snippets of wisdom
and foolishness; some contrived under
Bourbon, some from a great cigar,
but certainly a few with both!"*

✠

ADULT TONGUE TWISTER

Try not to quibble

whilst trying to say

"Nipple Nibble"

quickly three times in a row!

Nipple Nibble!

Nipple Nibble!

Nipple Nibble…!!

LOL!

❧

NIPPLE NIBBLE

"A *gentleman* **shall never**

quibble whilst *enjoying* a

Nipple Nibble!"

⚜

TO HEALTH

A friend once proclaimed that smoking and drinking were a danger to my health, to which I replied,

"So is dying, but right now it will have to wait until I finish this fine Bourbon and Cuban cigar!"

✦

TRADITION

"*I am the last lineage in creating this great* **tradition**.
Actually, I kind of started this **shit!**"

❧

SOCIAL MEDIA

"Your social media post should

contain an equal mix of

SARCASM,

HUMOR,

&

FACTS.

This way a proclamation can be

justified as any of the above."

MERCURY RETROGRADE

"When your life seems to be going backwards, might I suggest a simple shot of Bourbon. There are things that render Mercury retrograde quite irrelevant!"

DEGREES OF INTELLIGENCE

"The grasp of effective sarcasm requires a higher degree of intelligence from both the giver and receiver."

❦

SARCASM

"Do not judge my reply as mere

SARCASM

when its most obviously prose of

INTELLIGENT

REASONING."

⚜

TOLERANCE

"I find that

TOLERATING

the stupidity of others is easily

accomplished thru

SARCASTIC HUMOR

and a bit of

BOURBON!"

❧

UNFIT BEHAVIOR

"It's my wish that ridicule be sneered upon me for unfit behavior while I die from uncontrollable laughter!"

❧

DEPENDABLE

"It's just comforting to know there are things in life that we can depend on. The weatherman being wrong is such an example."

❧

WHAT HAPPENS IN VEGAS

"When the occasion calls for

libations and laughter,

be aware that the

Vegas Rule

shall apply."

COOKING

CAJUN PROTOCOL

"Catch it,

Kill it,

Clean it,

Cook it!"

THE EGG

"The EGG, while seemingly quite simple,

is one of the hardest of foods to MASTER.

A perfectly cooked EGG is a matter of preference,

thereby challenging the cook at EVERY CRACK!"

NIPPLE NIBBLE COCKTAIL

"A recipe to follow!"

The Nipple Nibble is a creamy cocktail designed to be savored. A gentleman slowly sips, enjoying each nibble experience, whilst the impatient novice shoots it.

Ingredients:
2 jiggers of good Bourbon for a real man, substitute with dark rum for everyone else!
2 jiggers heavy whipping cream
2 teaspoon dark brown sugar
1 tablespoon melted butter (salted)
pinch cayenne pepper
smidgeon of ground nutmeg
table salt to rim glasses

Preparation:
Rub a thin film of butter on the rim each glass and sprinkle lightly with salt. In large cocktail shaker, combine Bourbon,

cream, sugar, butter, and cayenne pepper. Shake vigorously for 30 seconds then slowly pour in cups to rim. Garnish each cup with a fresh raspberry carefully placed in center of glass upside-down. *Note: for saggy cups, substitute whipping cream with half & half.*

Served: Neat, perky, and always by the pair!

Yield: 2 "C" cups

Standard garnish: Fresh raspberry

For the Adventurous: Adjust recipe to 1 cup Bourbon, 1 cup heavy whipping cream, 2 tablespoons dark brown sugar, 6 tablespoons salted butter, ¼ teaspoon cayenne pepper, and pinch of ground nutmeg for a pair of "Double D" cups!

Drinkware: Shot glass for "C" cup, or Lowball glass DD" cup

KITCHEN GADGETS

"There are lots of kitchen gadgets that one who loves to cook can do without; alas my well-seasoned cast iron is not among them!"

❧

ART OF COOKING

"Cooking is the ultimate artistic expression

as it touches all five senses:

TOUCH,

SMELL,

TASTE,

SIGHT,

SOUND."

SPIRITUAL

✣

LIFE'S GIFTS

*"Blessings that are paid
forward are life's little gifts."*

BLESSED

"Blessed is he who takes the lone path
to aid another amongst the
crowd of onlookers."

BLIND FAITH

"Be not a

FOOL

by relying purely on

BLIND FAITH.

Miracles are made from the

application of God's greatest

gift to man;

REASON,

EFFORT,

&

DETERMINATION."

✠

TAKING ACTION

"Depending on prayer

&

blind faith alone

is foolish

when you have

the ability to act."

❦

HUMBLE

"OH YEA CASTERS OF THE FIRST STONE!
HUMBLE AM I IN YOUR MIST!"

❧

MOURNING

"If you lose a loved one,
mourn if you must, then set it aside.

Someone out there needs you."

HONORING A LOVED ONE

"The only way to fix mourning is to go out and be that person

you miss to someone else.

If you really love and miss them,

then you have a responsibility

to honor their memory by

being that person

for another."

EXPLAINING THE
PASSING OF MANY

"It's really not so unusual.

There are dying seasons if you will.

This time of year happens to be one of them.

As a lad, I served as an altar boy in our

church and regularly for funerals.

They always seemed to happen in waves

mainly at certain times of the year

for sick and elderly in particular.

We as a population take more

notice of those we know and

of public personalities.

Everyone else is just

Eleanor Rigby."

SPIRITS

"The spirit of those we love never die
or ever leave us.

Their memory is a reminder that
they are smiling upon us."

PRAYER

"Never seek miracles from the power of prayer,
instead ask for the gift of enlightenment to
guide you to the right path."

FORGIVENESS

"Forgiveness is the selfish act of relieving one's own burden, and while the struggle of giving it at times can seem unfathomable, it can never be denied or rejected!"

JUDGMENT

"Reserving judgments of those

ACCUSED

in wrongdoing spares regret when

FACTS

are revealed."

❧

CLOSURE

"Closure is the

GRATIFICATION

of lifting

BURDENS

we place on

OURSELVES.*"*

OPPORTUNITY

❦

CHAOS

"Live not in fear of chaos!
Thrive in its *opportunity!"*

CHASING DREAMS

"Helping others chase their
dreams is as rewarding
as pursuing your own."

DESPAIR

"Never give in to despair;

it clouds opportunity."

CAREER

❧

LABOR OF LOVE

"If you must labor, make it a labor of

LOVE,

else it will certainly harden your

HEART!"

❦

DRESSING THE PART

"In life, dressing for the part you are to

play isn't nearly as important as

dressing for the part you aspire to be."

SHARED VISION

"Even the best of intentions and
strong determination can be thwarted by those not
sharing the same vision for success."

❧

PERMISSION TO LEAD

"When looking for the opportunity

to excel in your career,

take on the most difficult of

problems, project, service, or delivery

that no one has answers for or wants."

OWNING A MISTAKE

"When faced with a
mistake you have made or
FAILURE
on your part, always accept responsibility
RIGHT AWAY
and state how you plan to
FIX IT.
This effectively
ENDS
the conversation and keeps it from being
USED AGAINST YOU."

✦

IMPOSSIBLE TASK

"When forced to

face what may be seen as an

impossible task

littered with obstacles,

one should envision the

desired outcome

because everything else is just

noise."

FOLLOWING THE MASSES

"In times of turmoil,
avoid blindly following
the masses as they are usually
wrong & misguided."

TRAVEL

*"My career has blessed me with the
opportunity to travel & live in many
places around the world.*

*I saw its beauty and plenty of its shame.
Both have made me a better man."*

LEADERSHIP

BIRTH OF A LEADER

"The birth of a leader is acting on the

natural instinct

of taking charge, accepting responsibility

without fear, hesitation, or permission,

all the while

earning respect

from those that follow."

TRUE LEADERSHIP

"True leadership is neither

EARNED, OR APPOINTED.

It is ceased by those with the courage to

STEP UP

in time of need or peril!"

❧

ACCEPTANCE

*"Leadership does not
require acceptance from others
to make bold decisions."*

INSPIRATION

LAUGHTER

"Laughter of an infant or child will soften the hardest of hearts!"

✚

FAITH IN MANKIND

"A single act of

kindness

can instantly

restore one's loss of

faith

in mankind."

❧

TRYING TIMES

"In trying times,

I remain

OPTIMISTIC;

in chaos,

INSPIRED!"

❧

WISE MAN

"A wise man wastes
no time with worry
as the pessimist amongst him
gladly accepts that burden."

JUDGMENTAL

"Admittedly

I am rather **judgmental.**

At first glance I only see the

best in **everyone."**

❧

OPPORTUNITY

"While some see crisis, I take time
to reflect in a proper
atmosphere and seek
out opportunity!"

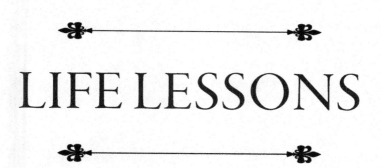

LIFE LESSONS

LIFE LESSONS

❧

GREATEST LESSON

**"Life's greatest lesson is one
learned the hard way."**

DEPTH OF CONVICTION

"None of us will ever know

the depth of our courage or honor

until being put to the test.

                    We can only pray

        that strength is bestowed upon us

                if ever faced with having

                to make that choice."

❧

OF MY LIFE

"I have done many things of which I am proud, and things that honestly I should be ashamed of. Yet, I make no apologies."

CHOICES

"My life is a reflection of decisions made and risks taken for good or bad.

No blame or credit is given for the circumstances except to the man staring back in the mirror."

"I AM MY CHOICES!"

❦

MY PURPOSE

"My purpose is to create a lasting space where people gather to share knowledge, wisdom, love, and abundance!'

VOYAGES

"I never dreamed for any of this. I do what I must and find a way to make the very best of it all!

I would rather be eating gumbo and crawfish in south Louisiana but such is life. Never be jealous of another's life since you have not walked in their shoes.

Instead, create great memories of your own. Perfect moments in time require no travel."

LOOKING BACK

"I make no apologies for the life I have lived or the choices made for they have shaped the man I have become for good or bad.

For any whom I may have wronged or slighted in the past, know that forgiveness is yours alone to give. I hold no such burden as mine is given freely to all.

For those who positively impacted my life, know that there are no words that could adequately express my gratitude.

Simply - *Thank You!*"

❦

FRIENDSHIP

"Some of the greatest of life's friendships
are formed from a passion of a common
interest by those who otherwise would be
torn apart thru opposing viewpoints of
deeply held beliefs."

❦

REPUTATION

"Reputation bestowed upon one by others comes from their own life choices."

❧

TO PARENTS

"The very best of our parents lives is a reflection of who we have become!"

PHILISOPHY

❧

FINE CIGAR

"The world's

finest cigar

is the one enjoyed in the

company of friends."

❦

CONFUCIUS-ISM

*"Foot in mouth is often cured
with bad taste left from sole!"*

❧

SHIT HAPPENS

"**S**HIT HAPPENS,
YET WISDOM ENDURES!"

FILLING THE GLASS

"While there are those that

DEBATE

whether the glass is half full or empty,

my attention is turned to

FINDING MORE GLASSES

to pour drink for those that

FULFILL MY LIFE."

LIFE'S JOURNEY

"LIFE'S A JOURNEY.

Restlessness is just a part of seeking greater

KNOWLEDGE.

Only those content with mediocrity

BELIEVE

in true happiness."

STOKING PASSIONS

The relentless pursuit of one's favorite

pass time or hobby can either lead

to its perfection or missed opportunity

to expand ones experience."

✣

ACCEPTING DEFEAT

"Loss of hope
is one of
accepting
defeat."

❧

NOTHING TO LOSE

"*Those who **publically proclaim** they have*

nothing to lose are also

*likely **mistaken** into the*

*belief they have **much to gain.**"*

DARWIN

"Politicians keep passing laws that thwart Darwin's

survival of the fittest,

so we have become stuck with the

lesser amongst us!"

GIVING UP

"People are far more likely to give up on themselves long before others do regardless of how others actually perceive them."

DIGNITY

"To witness the loss of

ones dignity

because they

stubbornly overstay

their welcome or position

is perhaps not worthy of

another's pity."

⚜

SELFISH

"Those who cannot give or share unconditionally
are really seeking either accolades
or pity from
others."

AGING

❦

CALENDAR

"It's just a calendar I say;

you should strive to be a

better person every day."

✤

YOUTHFULNESS

"You may not be as

old

as you look, but you are certainly as

young

as you feel!"

OVER THE HILL

"It's not the top of the hill;

its just a place where

you see a different purpose in life.

While seeking greater enlightenment,

only you can choose the path downhill;

after all it is your journey."

✦

BUCKET LIST

"Life is short, love and live large.
Smile and make laughter for many.
May you finish life never knowing
Your bucket has a hole in it!"

CENTENARIAN

"Long ago I decided I would live

to the age of **100 years!***"*

"While some scoff at

the merits of such a proclamation,

I sometimes wonder whether the goal

was a bit short on **optimism!***"*

❦

STARTING OVER

"It's never too late.

STARTING OVER & SECOND CHANCES

have the same expiration date

AS LIFE ITSELF."

PROCLAMATION

SOUNDS OF YESTERYEAR

"*There is nothing as*
SOOTHING
as the imperfect sounds
produced by a needle
working the grooves of
VINYL."

MANNERS

"While the loss of

proper manners

is disheartening,

that it would become a

Southern trait

is a tragedy!"

DIVERSITY

"Diversity of opinion is not a hindrance,

but an expansion of one's own knowledge."

❧

ENCOURAGING OTHERS

"You never really know when words of

ENCOURAGEMENT

may have such an impact that it could make a

LIFE ALTERING

change for another."

FUN

"Even in the direst of moments,

one can still choose to have fun!"

KEEPING GOOD COMPANY

"They say the measure
of a man can be foretold
by the company he keeps.

Thanks to my circle of friends,
I AM A RICH MAN.

Alas, the true character
of a man is formed
by the women that
surrounds his life!"

LEARNING FROM MISTAKES

"What is important in life
is that you learn from your mistakes,
especially the ones you make over and over!"

MORE

"Nothing in life was ever

ACHIEVED

without asking for

MORE."

❧

MISTAKES

"Making mistakes aren't nearly
as bad as not learning from them."

❧

FALLACY OF EQUALITY

"IF EQUALITY

were to be achieved amongst peoples,

they would never

PROGRESS

beyond the lowest common denominator!"

REJECTING HATE

"*Never* hate stupid people!"

"They allow you to look like a *genius* even when

you make mistakes!"

TIGHT LIPPED

"It's better to hold your opinion when a fool speaks,
than allow the appearance of a second fool!"

COMMITMENT

"I generally find that people
who feel the need to publicly express
their intent to make a
major change in their life or
in the way they do things,
have no commitment to do so.

Real change comes from action,
not acknowledgement from others."

CRAZY

"Some mistake *crazy* for *unique*.

It's not their fault

of course

as they are just no

different than the *masses*.

Remain crazy – *it's the sane thing to do!*"

FOOLS

✤

FOOL

"Never quote a

fool

least they may somehow

assume their point is

valid."

WORTHLESS OPINION

"While I find your opinions
entertaining
they are nonetheless useless."

❧

OFFEND

"Should my comments offend you or be deemed
in some way inappropriate, no relief will be
found from questioning my reasoning for
saying so!"

✦

SILENCE

"So much comes to mind

that should be said, yet it's the

SILENCE

that deems it all

INAPPROPRIATE."

RELEVANCE

" Foolishness and stupidity

are only given relevance

because it is acknowledged

instead of ignored."

❦

GRAVE CONCERN

*"It's not so much the **opinions** of those viewed as foolish that concerns me."*
*"It is the worry that they might indeed **vote** or **procreate!**"*

JEALOUSY

"Your low self-esteem *&* feelings of

inferiority

are not somehow

alleviated

by accusing others of

acting

like they are better than yourself."

FEAR

"Have no fear of the

STUPIDITY *&* **OPINIONS**

of the masses, instead relish in the

OPPORTUNITY

it will present!"

SNOWFLAKES

"In the world of business,

it's going to get easier to

compete & market

to the lesser of us."

❦

WINNERS AND LOSERS

"It is comforting to know when

life separates

winners from losers

in survival of the fittest,

wins can be easily had

given today's competition."

✦

SIMPLE STATEMENT

"If you did not understand

my point the first time,

a detailed explanation

won't help since you are unable to

grasp a

simple

statement."

❧

SEEKING LOGIC

"Seeking logic from the unexplainable
actions of others can encourage
people to question
your sanity."

POLITICAL
RANT

PROTEST

"Being paid to show up in defiance of an

issue is disturbing the peace, not protest."

❧

RIGHT TO VOTE

"With the right to vote comes

RESPONSIBILITY.

Casting a ballot purely on

SEX, RACE, OR THE RELIGION

of a candidate is irresponsible.

Be accountable and choose wisely!"

VOTING

"If not voting because you think it nether matters, makes no difference, or counts; the same holds true of your opinions."

"Spare those of us who respect the process the emptiness of your thoughts!"

❦

HYPOCRISY

"Imagine the hypocrisy of those that

bemoan capitalism as 'evil',

all the while being fattened from its

bounty taken from those that

earned it and given to them freely!"

✤

ARGUING FACTS

"The fallacy that one could destroy

a liberal's argument

is the false assumption

that facts would actually matter."

WHITE PRIVILEGE

"Yep! You liberal apologists keep fretting over white privilege for us!

We are too busy making a living and taking care of our families to stop and look in the mirror to see the that which you bestowed upon us.

In the meantime, you can go feeling justified till we have time in our lives to care enough to dispute those claims!

Carry on you fools! Am off to go to work to earn that undeserving white privilege!"

GLOBAL PERCEPTION

"Most people around the globe base their perceptions about United States of America and its politics from what they learn in the news media.

Those are generally biased towards one slant or other, or just outright propaganda by their own governments.

While some complaints are valid, America is in a unique position as the government still works for the people not the other way around as in most places.

Regardless of what the rest of the world thinks or wants, America's strength and greatness comes from the Constitution and its Amendments.

It is the amazing gift from the brilliance and foresight of our Founding Fathers!"

❧

ILLUSION OF
"HOPE AND CHANGE"

America should prepare itself for more riots and civil unrest as the illusion of a better life by those that believed the lie slowly fades away.

What was once "Hope and Change"will turn to despair and anger.

The voices of those who perpetuated the lie will grow louder as they cease the opportunity to divide the nation further for their own selfish gain.

Inside America cries for a real leader to emerge to steer this great nation back to The Constitution and its Amendments as prescribed by our Forefathers!

❧

TO THE UNITED NATIONS

"Be it known unto all men!"

"I, Shane John Meche,
                     citizen and patriot of the great
                                      United States of America,

recognizes no law, treaty, policy, pact, or outright
legitimacy of the sham that is the United Nations,

nor do I endorse or approve of any actions of the
Executive, Legislative, or Judicial branches of the
United States to do so on my behalf or behalf of my
family that would in any way alter, impair, remove,
or subvert any and all rights granted to me at
birth by the Constitution of the United States
and its Amendments in place at that time."

DEADLY ASSOCIATIONS

"Please note,

due to reoccurring

MYSTERIOUS DEATHS,

I have no

PERSONAL, BUSINESS, OR POLITICAL

relationship with the Clintons!"

BY OTHERS

IMPORTANT READING

This section contains material which in my opinion is important to read and understand for Citizens, Patriots, and those residing in the United States of America:

- Magna Carta
- Declaration of Independence
- Constitution of the United States
- Bill of Rights

INFLUENTIAL BOOKS

Each of the books below provided influence and valuable guidance in my life as well as countless others.

- "The King James Bible"
- "A Wealth of Nations" by Adam Smith
- "Atlas Shrugged" by Ayn Rand
- "The Republic" by Plato
- "Nineteen Eighty-Four" by George Orwell
- "The Art of War" by Sun Tzu
- "How to Win Friends and Influence People," by Dale Carnegie
- "Think and Grow Rich" by Napoleon Hill
- "The Richest Man in Babylon" by George S. Clason
- "Good to Great" by Jim Collins
- "Civil Disobedience" by Henry David Thoreau

THE TEN COMMANDMENTS

I.   I am the Lord thy God and thou shalt not have other gods before me.

II.   Thou shalt not make for thyself any graven image.

III. Thou shalt not take the name of the Lord thy God in vain.

IV.   Remember the Lord's Day to keep it holy.

V.   Honor thy Father and Mother.

VI.   Thou shalt not kill.

VII. Thou shalt not commit adultery.

VIII. Thou shalt not steal.

IX.   Thou shalt not bear false witness against thy neighbor.

X.   Thou shalt not covet thy neighbor's goods.

PSALM 23

The Lord is my shepherd; I shall not want.

He maketh me to lie down in green pastures; He leadeth me beside the still waters.

He restoreth my soul; He leadeth me in the paths of righteousness for His name's sake.

Yea, though I walk through the valley of the shadow of death, I will fear no evil; for Thou art with me; Thy rod and Thy staff, they comfort me.

Thou preparest a table before me in the presence of mine enemies; Thou anointest my head with oil; my cup runneth over.

Surely goodness and mercy shall follow me all the days of my life; and I will dwell in the house of the Lord forever.

❦

DON'T QUIT

When things go wrong, as they sometimes will,

    When the road you're trudging seems all uphill,

When the funds are low and the debts are high,

    And you want to smile, but you have to sigh,

When care is pressing you down a bit-

    Rest if you must, but don't you quit.

Life is queer with its twists and turns,

    As every one of us sometimes learns,

And many a fellow turns about

    When he might have won had he stuck it out.

Don't give up though the pace seems slow -

    You may succeed with another blow.

Often the goal is nearer than

    It seems to a faint and faltering man;

Often the struggler has given up

When he might have captured the victor's cup;

And he learned too late when the night came down,

How close he was to the golden crown.

Success is failure turned inside out -

The silver tint in the clouds of doubt,

And you never can tell how close you are,

It might be near when it seems afar;

So stick to the fight when you're hardest hit -

It's when things seem worst that you must not quit.

~AUTHOR UNKNOWN

AFTERWORD

In the earliest days of the internet and the introduction of web pages, all sorts of ideas were tried in an effort to find use for this newfound technology. One such idea was that of a poetry aggregation site which sent out a promotional email to get users to its site.

As I recall, they had some sort of promotion to entice viewers to submit a poem with the possibility of it becoming published. For whatever reason, I decided to give it a shot, and a quick idea was typed out without much thought. After acknowledgement that my submission was received, it dawned on me that what I had just written was pretty good, yet I had no copy of it! Since sites at the time were fairly crude, I found no way to retrieve what had been written and soon those thoughts were forgotten.

A few months later, a letter arrived in the mail from the poetry site offering to publish my poem, and of course, I could also purchase a copy of the book as well as a few other "upsell" items lined out in the offering. While the purchase of a poetry book was readily dismissed, the letter did contain the words that I had hastily written that day many months before.

After thinking it was lost forever, "A New Day" by Shane Meche was found printed in this mailing and thus started that habit of keeping a copy of writings no matter how trivial.

My second poem, "Mi Luna", was written over my fascination with Solunar Theory and the effects that the moon has on our lives.

Most of the writings contained in this book were inspired by current events or individuals present in my life at the time of their creation.

The Political Rant section of the book clearly contains writings that will not appeal to, or be appreciated by all who read this. While it is not the intention of this section change minds or rally others, they were important enough at the time to write down, therefore important enough to include in the book.

Illusion of "Hope and Change" was a writing of my thoughts nearing end the first term of Barrack Obama as President of the United States. Sadly, little did I know at the time of just how true those words would become. America had become hopelessly divided and partisan to the likes which I had not previously seen in my lifetime.

AUTHOR'S BIO

Shane Meche is a bestselling author of corporate industry assignments with his work appearing in numerous telecommunication infrastructure documents, convincing presentations, and "let's just go ahead and reply to all" email summaries from the copy-edit-paste profession of global business consulting. As a distinguished professor from the University of Hard Knocks, School of Southern Gentlemen, Shane pushes unsolicited advice, questionable wisdom, cloaked sarcasm, and unabashed humor to any who dare listen.

When displaced from the world of taxable income generation, he enjoys the art of cooking and fine dining, entertaining of friends and family, harvesting fish and game in the great outdoors, idea creation to product design, as well as scribbling his thoughts while pondering life's nuisances. These of course are usually accompanied by laughter, good Bourbon, and a fine cigar.

CONNECT WITH SHANE

WEBSITE: ShaneMeche.com
EMAIL: shane@shanemeche.com

CPSIA information can be obtained
at www.ICGtesting.com
Printed in the USA
LVOW13*1323170618
580680LV00001B/3/P